Love to Sew

Patchwork Bags

Love to Sew

Patchwork Bags

Cecilia Hanselmann

Search Press

First published in Great Britain 2013 by Search Press Limited
Wellwood, North Farm Road, Tunbridge Wells, Kent TN2 3DR

Reprinted 2014 (twice)

Original German edition published as *Patchwork Taschen*

Copyright © 2012 Christophorus Verlag GmbH,
Freiburg/Germany

English translation by Burravoe Translation Services

ISBN: 978-1-84448-927-5

Designs and production: Dagmar Clever (page 52–53),
Claudia Hager (page 16–18), Handicraft Work (page 54–56),
Cecilia Hanselmann (page 14–15, 28–29, 40–43, 47–49,
60–63), Creative Ideas (page 44–46), Bärbel Jankowski
(page 50–51), Ute Klunk (page 57–59), Desiree Köllner (page
19–21, 34–36), Bea Matzek (page 37–39), Kerstin Porsch
(page 25–27), Angelika Schwinn (page 30–33), Heike Ziefuß
(page 22–24)

Photography and styling: Uwe Bick/Karin Schlag,
Uli Glasemann/Elke Reith (page 14–15, 28–29, 40–43,
47–49, 60–63)

Technical drawings: OZ archive, Claudia Schmidt

The manufacturers mentioned in this book refer to those
organisations that kindly supplied the materials and
equipment used by the author. Many of these organisations
provide on-line ordering facilities and distribute worldwide.
However, all of the materials and equipment used in this
book can be readily obtained from alternative sources,
including specialist stores, on-line suppliers and
mail-order companies.

Printed in China

Make-up Pouch, page 14

Sea of Flowers, page 16

Sea Breeze, page 25

Summer Spots, page 28

Fun and Flirty, page 37

Dynamic Duo, page 40

Just for Fun, page 52

Rose Windows, page 54

Contents

Home is Where the Heart is, page 19

Spring is in the Air, page 22

Favourite Wash Bag, page 30

Red Retro, page 34

On Your Travels, page 44

Heavenly Hexagons, page 47

Uniquely You, page 50

Traveller's Friend, page 57

Summer Bag, page 60

Summer Purse, page 62

Introduction

Welcome to the wonderful world of bags. You can find the perfect bag for any occasion here, from a shopping bag or travel holdall to a handy purse, and because you are making the bag yourself, you can choose whatever colours and patterns you like to make the bag unique and perfect for you – it is your choice.

   Each project is graded according to difficulty and many of the designs are suitable for beginners. The instructions take you through the bag-making process in easy stages, and all the basic techniques required are explained at the beginning of the book to help you further. If you are a more confident sewer, you may like to make modifications to your chosen bag. For example, you could add or omit an inside pocket or a key holder, and if you prefer a different strap or handle on your bag, or a different way of attaching it, then just take inspiration from another project in the book – enjoy being creative and, above all, have fun with your sewing.

Sewing basics

Templates and patterns

Many of the bags in this book are made from simple rectangles, squares or strips of fabric and you will be given the dimensions in the 'Cutting out' sections accompanying each project. Sometimes you will require a pattern, and these are provided on the folded pattern sheet at the back of the book. It is best to trace the patterns on to thin paper, transferring the markings as well, when required. The embroidery pattern for the bag on page 22 is provided in mirror image so that it will be the right way round when you transfer it to your fabric.

Ironing

Iron the fabrics before cutting out and after sewing each seam. Take care with synthetic or delicate fabrics; to be safe, cover these with a clean cotton cloth and iron over the cloth. Do the same with any embroidery. In order to simplify the instructions and avoid repetition, ironing is not always mentioned in the individual projects.

Fabric grain

All woven fabric is made up of warp threads (lengthways) and weft threads (widthways). The grain corresponds to the direction of the warp threads and runs parallel to the selvedge. Cut the pattern pieces so that they run parallel to the warp and weft threads. Pieces cut on the bias – diagonally across the grain – will easily stretch out of shape.

Cutting out

Cutting out accurately is vital to the success of your project. For straight-sided pieces, measure carefully and then check your measurement before cutting out. When using a pattern, first trace the shape carefully on to thin paper and then cut out. Pin the paper pattern to the wrong side of the fabric and draw around it using tailor's chalk or a fabric marker pen. Add the relevant seam allowance all around, if required, then cut out the shape with a sharp pair of scissors or a rotary cutter on a cutting mat. You can buy special circle cutters to cut perfect circles for rosettes or draw around a suitable object such as a glass.

Cutting on the fold

Some pattern pieces need to be cut on the fold. To do this, simply fold the fabric along the grain and place the pattern on top with the broken line on the pattern placed directly on the fabric fold. Cut out the fabric through both layers, ideally using a cutting mat and rotary cutter.

Right and wrong sides of the fabric

Every fabric has a right and a wrong side. The right side is the side that is on display, or the outside of the fabric. With patterned fabrics, this is really easy to recognise because the pattern is clearer. So, when it says 'lay the pieces of fabric right sides together', the right sides will be on the inside and the wrong sides will face outwards. Sometimes the difference between the two sides of the fabric is as simple as a change of sheen or grain. If you are unable to distinguish the right and wrong sides of the fabric, you can use either side.

Tacking and pinning

Always pin the fabric pieces before sewing and then tack by hand. This prevents the fabric layers from slipping when they are being sewn and prevents unwanted wrinkles.

Seam allowance

If a fabric is sewn too close to the edge, the fabric and the seam will easily tear apart but if the seam allowance is too wide it creates bulk in the finished item. Seam allowances for the projects in this book are usually 0.75 cm (¼in) or 1cm (⅜in). The width of the seam allowance is stated in the instructions under 'Cutting out'.

Thread tension

The tension on the sewing machine must be adjusted to suit the type of fabric, otherwise loops can occur in the bottom or top threads. It is best to assess the tension on a test piece first.

Straight stitch

Straight stitch is the basic sewing-machine stitch and is the stitch to use unless otherwise stated in the instructions. The stitch length can be adjusted – the longer the stitch, the looser the seam will be.

Zigzag stitch

This is used to neaten raw edges. The width and length of the stitch can be adjusted. A very narrow zigzag stitch can also be used to appliqué a motif or fabric shape on to another piece of fabric.

Sewing kit

These basic items are required for each of the projects in this book:

- ♥ Sewing machine
- ♥ Dressmakers' pins
- ♥ Tailor's chalk
- ♥ Seam ripper
- ♥ Cutting mat, ruler and rotary cutter
- ♥ Matching sewing thread
- ♥ Small embroidery scissors
- ♥ Dressmakers' scissors
- ♥ Tape measure
- ♥ Sewing needles
- ♥ Pattern paper
- ♥ Pen
- ♥ Iron and ironing board

Techniques

Finishing seams

Seams should be secured at each end to prevent them from coming apart. To start, stitch three to four stitches forwards, then stitch backwards over the stitches just made and then stitch the seam. Reverse over your stitches at the end of the seam in the same way.

Stitching curved seams

Stitch curved seams parallel to the fabric edge. Before turning out, clip the seam allowances at short intervals almost to the stitching, as shown. This will prevent lumpy seams after turning out. On extreme curves and angles you can cut small wedges out of the seam allowance to reduce bulk further.

Oversewing

This hand stitch is used for closing up an opening left for turning a piece right side out. Stitch as shown, working small stitches vertically. Knot the thread securely at each end to prevent unravelling.

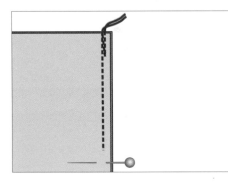 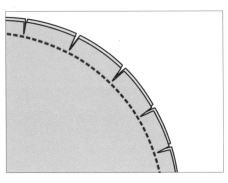 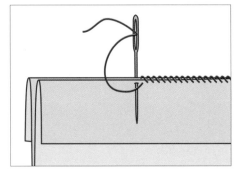

Inserting a zip

1 Stitch the seam as far as the opening for the zip fastener and press the seam allowances open. If necessary, tack the seam where the zip will go to hold it in place. This is important for long zips.

2 Insert the zipper foot into the sewing machine. Turn the piece right side up and pin or tack the zip fastener beneath the opening. Sew the first side of the zip fastener close to the zip teeth.

3 At the bottom of the zip, leave the needle in the fabric, raise the presser foot, turn the piece and then lower the foot. Sew straight across the seam to the other side. Pivot the fabric with the needle down as before and then topstitch up second side.

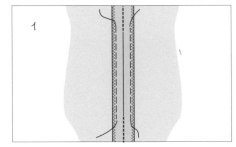 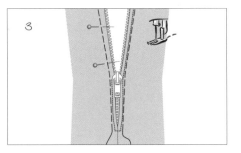

Making tabs or loops

1 Sew the strips for the tabs or loops along one long edge, across the end and then along the other long edge, right sides together. Trim the seam allowances at corners diagonally, close to the stitches but not quite touching them. For a pointed tab, stitch as shown above right and trim off the excess fabric to reduce bulk.

2 To create a tab, loop or handle with a curved end, first shape the end using a suitable curved object as a template and trim the fabric. Stitch the seam. Snip into the seam allowances, taking out small wedges of fabric, as shown in the diagram below.

Shaping the base

To create the box shape at the bottom of a bag, fold the side seams or side folds over the seam or fold at the bottom of the bag. This will create a triangular shape. Stitch a short seam at right angles to the bottom fold the specified distance from the corner point. Trim off the excess fabric and zigzag the raw edges.

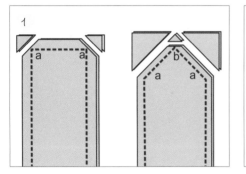

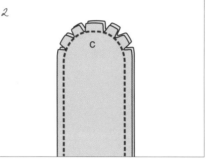

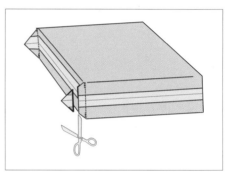

Making straps and handles

1 Fold each strip in half lengthways, wrong sides together and edges matching. Iron the fold to press the crease. Unfold the strip and then fold in both the long edges to meet at the centre fold. Press again.

2 Fold in half lengthways again. You now have four layers of fabric plus any wadding or interfacing the project may require. Topstitch along both long edges unless stated otherwise in the project instructions.

Making a rosette

Take a circle of fabric and roll a small seam allowance to the wrong side of the fabric using your finger and thumb. Using a matching double thread, work running stitch all around the edge, securing the beginning with a knot and a backstitch. Pull up the thread so that the circle gathers together. Tie off the thread.

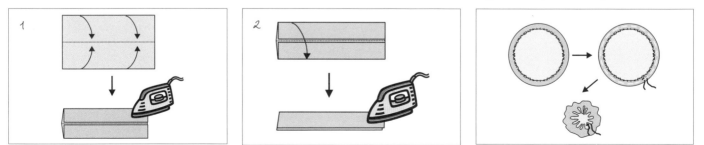

Machine appliqué

Fusible webbing

This is an invaluable product when working with appliqué. Essentially it is a fine sheet of fabric glue with a protective sheet of paper on each side. Remove the paper from one side so you can fuse it to fabric. You can draw your pattern on the paper backing to use as a template. Once fused to fabric, the webbing helps to prevent fraying. This product is sold under several brand names including Bondaweb and Fuse-a-Web.

Preparation

Designs for appliqué can be traced from books, magazines, fabrics, other items or you can design your own. You can even scan them into a computer and modify them or enlarge or reduce them on a photocopier before transferring them to the webbing.

1 First trace your appliqué motifs on to the fusible web in mirror image so that they will be the right way round when the fabric is cut out. (If the pattern is symmetrical you do not have to worry about this.)

2 Trace each motif individually and then roughly cut out the fusible web around it. For complicated designs, number the appliqué pieces to help keep track of what goes where.

Fusing the layers

3 Remove the backing from the webbing and iron the shapes on to the wrong side of the appliqué fabric, with the backing paper on top and the fusible web directly on the fabric. Apply the iron carefully using the heat setting recommended by the webbing manufacturer. Leave the pieces to cool and then cut out precisely around the drawn lines of the motifs.

4 Remove the backing paper from the pieces and arrange on the right side of background fabric, following your chosen design. Make sure that the pieces are in the correct order. A needle or pin can be useful to help prise the backing paper from the webbing.

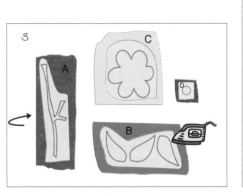

For complicated designs, make sure you place the bottom pieces first and overlapping pieces on top.

Stitching the layers

First back the fabric with stabiliser to help prevent puckering. You can use a cut-away, tear-away or wash-away version. This is not essential, but it will help to produce the best results.

Usually, when sewing appliqué, machine embroidery thread is used as the top thread. This is less tightly spun than normal sewing thread and can therefore spread out flatter, giving a smooth and dense appearance to the stitching. For the bottom thread, a universal bobbin thread for embroidery is suitable or sewing thread in a colour to match the top thread. An open presser foot can be very useful for appliqué work because it enables you to have a good view of the raw edge of the piece

to be attached. Use a dense zigzag stitch (stitch length 1mm, stitch width 2-3mm) for sewing on the appliqué, or a machine appliqué stitch or small, straight stitch close to the raw edge. Most appliqués are sewn using a dense zigzag stitch because this gives the outlines a slightly 3-D effect and hides the raw fabric edges. Test the desired stitch first and, if necessary, loosen the tension of the top thread a little so that the loop formation of the upper and lower threads falls on the back of the fabric. Transfer any lines inside the individual appliqué pieces on to the fabric using a marker pen and oversew using zigzag or straight stitch. Once the appliqué is complete, remove the stabiliser.

8

Materials

Cotton fabric:
- 25cm (10in) red fabric with white spots, 10cm (44in) wide
- about 30 different colourful fabric remnants each at least 6.5 x 3–9cm (2½ x 1¼–3½in)

Wadding:
- 20 x 90cm (8 x 35½in) fusible wadding

Additional item:
- one white zip fastener, 20cm (8in) long

Preparation

Make a template for the pouch using the pattern on sheet A. Add a 0.75cm (¼in) seam allowance all round.

Cutting out

The following measurements include a 0.75cm (¼in) seam allowance.

Spotted fabric:
- 4 strips, 5 x 21.5cm (2 x 8½in), for the top band and its facing
- 2 pouches, using the pattern on sheet A, for the lining

Fabric remnants:
- approximately 30 rectangles, each 6.5cm (2½in) wide and 3–9cm (1¼–3½in) long
- 4.5 x 31.5cm (1¾ x 12½in) strip for the strap

Fusible wadding:
- 4 strips, 5 x 21.5cm (2 x 8½in)
- 2 pouches, using the pattern on sheet A

Make-up Pouch

Wrist bag   **Size:** 16.5 x 24cm (6½ x 13½in)   Pattern sheet A   **Level of difficulty** ♡

Sewing

1 Sew the remnant rectangles together along the 6.5cm (2½in) edges to form strips about 30cm (12in) long. Sew the strips together along the long edges to make a large rectangle. From this, cut two pouches using the pattern. Now fuse the corresponding wadding to the back of each one. Fuse wadding to the wrong side of two of the spotted strips for the top bands.

2 With right sides facing, sew one wadded top band to the top edge of each wadded pouch piece. Press the seam allowances towards the top band then topstitch in place, close to the seam on the top band.

3 Join each remaining top band (without wadding) to the top of each spotted pouch piece, stitching with right sides facing. Press the seam. These pieces will be the lining.

4 Place the zip flush with the top edge of one wadded pouch piece, on the top band, with right sides facing. Pin a lining on top, right side down, with edges matching, then stitch along the zip edge using the zip foot on your machine. Open out the fabric pieces and fold wrong sides together, matching the raw edges. Topstitch close to the zip teeth on the right side; press carefully. Repeat for the other side of the zip.

5 Make the strap as described on page 11, topstitching both of the long edges close to the folds. Fold the strap in half and zigzag the short ends together.

Assembly

1 Tack the strap ends flush with the side edge of the top band on one wadded pouch piece, with the main part of the strap resting on the right side of the band. Arrange the pouch pieces right sides together, lining against lining and patchwork against patchwork. Sew together around the edge, leaving a gap of about 10cm (4in) in the lining section for turning out.

2 Turn the pouch right sides out, pushing the seams out well. Sew up the opening in the lining with small hand stitches and press the bag lightly. Arrange the lining in the pouch.

Sea of Flowers

Summer bag   Size: approximately 30 x 34cm (12 x 13½in)   **Level of difficulty** ♡

Materials

Cotton fabric, about 110cm (44in) wide:
- 70cm (¾yd) border fabric in turquoise/blue/green for the bag
- 35cm (½yd) coordinating cotton fabric for the lining

Wadding and interfacing:
- 45 x 90cm (17¾ x 35½in) fusible wadding
- 20 x 90cm (8 x 35½in) firm fusible pelmet interfacing

Cutting out

The following measurements include a 1cm (³⁄₈in) seam allowance.

Main fabric:
- 2 rectangles 30 x 44cm (12 x 17¼in) for the front and back
- 4 strips 7 x 33cm (2½ x 13in) for the top band and its facing
- 2 strips 12 x 80cm (4¾ x 31½in) for the handles

Lining fabric:
- 2 rectangles 30 x 44cm (12 x 17¼in) for the lining. Trim a wedge shape off each side of the piece so that the top edge is 33cm (13in), the bottom edge is 44cm (17¼in) and the height is 30cm (12in). The finished shape must be symmetrical.

Firm fusible pelmet interfacing:
- 2 strips 5.5 x 78cm (2¼ x 30¾in) for the handles
- 2 strips 5 x 31cm (2 x 12¼in) for the top band

Fusible wadding:
- 2 rectangles 28 x 42cm (11 x 16½in). Trim each rectangle as before so that the top edge is 31cm (12¼in), the bottom edge is 42cm (16½in) and the height is 28cm (11in) – the padding is smaller than the lining fabric all round.
- 2 strips 5.5 x 78cm (2¼ x 30¾in) for the handles
- 2 strips 5 x 31cm (2 x 12¼in) for the top band

When cutting out the border fabric, make sure that the strips for the handles and top band are cut from the relevant sections of the fabric.

Sewing

1 Starting in the centre of the 44cm (17¼in) top edge of each front/back rectangle, and working towards the sides, make pleats so that the pleated edge is 33cm (13in) wide. Tack the folds in place.

2 Iron a 5 x 31cm (2 x 12¼in) strip of wadding to the wrong side of two top-band strips, and iron a 5 x 31cm (2 x 12¼in) strip of pelmet interfacing to the wrong side of each of the remaining two top-band strips. Sew a wadded strip to the top edges of the front and back pieces and an interfaced strip to the top edge of each of the lining pieces. Remove the tacking stitches.

3 Iron a shaped piece of wadding centrally to the wrong side of each corresponding lining piece. The fabric is 1cm (³⁄₈in) larger all round than the wadding.

4 Fold each handle strip in half lengthways and press to mark the centre then unfold. Iron a corresponding strip of wadding to one half of the strip, so one edge is at the fold line, and iron a strip of pelmet interfacing to the other half of the strip in the same way. There should be a seam allowance around the edge. Fold the excess fabric on the long sides on to the wadding/interfacing and press. Fold the strips in half, wrong sides together, along the pressed fold, and topstitch each long edge. Zigzag across the ends to secure.

5 Lay one pleated bag piece on a lining piece, right sides together, so that the top bands match. Lay a handle between the layers of fabric, placing the ends on the top seam about 4.5cm (1¾in) away from the sides, with the loop of the handle pointing downwards between the layers. Sew the top edge of the top band, catching the handles in the seam. Repeat to attach the other handle to the other bag pieces. Open out the layers of fabric and place the bag pieces together with right sides facing, matching the lining pieces together and the bag pieces together. The pieces for the top band must match each other too. Sew around the outside edges, leaving a gap at the base of the lining for turning out. Do not turn out yet.

6 To shape the base, push one side seam of the bag on to the bottom seam. This will form a triangle (see page 11). Stitch across the triangle at right angles to the seam, 4cm (1¾in) away from the point. Trim off the excess fabric. Repeat with other bag side seam and then with the lining.

7 Now turn the bag out through the opening in the lining, close the opening with small hand stitches and push the lining into the bag. Topstitch the top edge of the bag.

If you wish to make inside pockets from the fabric remnants, then these must be sewn to the right side of the lining pieces before assembly (see, for example, the clutch bag on page 37).

Home is Where the Heart is

Spacious holdall   **Size:** approximately 32 x 46cm (12½ x 18in)   **Level of difficulty** ♡

Materials

Cotton fabric, about 110cm (44in) wide:
- 45cm (½yd) red striped cotton
- 45cm (½yd) red checked cotton

Wadding and interfacing:
- 55 x 90cm (21¾ x 35½in) fusible wadding
- 55 x 90cm (21¾ x 35½in) firm fusible pelmet interfacing

Additional items:
- heart appliqué motif
- 80cm (1yd) white insertion lace, 4.5cm (1¾in) wide
- 30cm (12in) white lace edging, 7cm (2¾in) wide
- 1 pair of bag handles, 60cm (24in) long
- 2 decorative buttons

Cutting out

The following measurements include a 1cm (⅜in) seam allowance.

Red striped cotton:
- 2 rectangles 37 x 49cm (14½ x 19¼in) for the front/back (the stripes should run parallel to the short edge)
- 4 strips 6 x 10cm (2¼ x 4in) for the handle loops

Red checked cotton:
- 40 x 96cm (16 x 37¾in) rectangle for the lining
- 37 x 24cm (14½ x 9½in) rectangle for the centre front
- 4 strips 4 x 10cm (1½ x 4in) for the handle loops

Fusible wadding:
- 2 rectangles 37 x 49cm (14½ x 19¼in)

Firm, fusible pelmet interfacing:
- 2 rectangles 37 x 49cm (14½ x 19¼in)

Insertion lace:
- 2 pieces 37cm (14½in) long

Sewing

1 Appliqué the heart to the centre of the 37 x 24cm (14½ x 9½in) rectangle of checked fabric. Pin this centrally on to one of the large striped rectangles with right sides facing up. Pin a strip of insertion lace either side of it, covering the raw edges of the checked piece. Topstitch along each long edge of the insertion lace, catching the checked piece in the stitching.

2 Fuse a piece of wadding and then interfacing to the wrong side of each of the striped rectangles. Quilt the pieces as desired. Pin the rectangles right sides together and sew along both short edges and the lower long edge. Neaten all the fabric edges with zigzag stitch.

3 To shape the base of the bag, push one side seam inside on to the base seam, so the seams match. This will form a triangle at the side (see page 11). Stitch across the triangle at right angles to the seam, 4cm (1½in) away from the point. Trim off the excess fabric and neaten the raw edges with zigzag stitch. Repeat on the other side. Turn the bag out and tack the lace edging to the top edge of the bag.

4 Fold the long edges of each checked strip to the centre, wrong sides together, and press. Repeat with the striped strips. Centre a checked strip on each striped one so that the neat sides are facing out. Topstitch along the long edges of the checked strips. Thread a strip through each wooden ring on the bag handles to form loops. Tack the ends of the loops flush with the top of the bag on the right side, so each one is about 12cm (4¾in) from the side of the bag.

5 Fold the remaining checked rectangle in half horizontally, with right sides facing, and stitch each side edge. Shape the base as you did for the bag and neaten all the fabric edges with zigzag stitch to prevent fraying. Do not turn out the lining.

Assembly

Place the lining into the bag with wrong sides together. Turn down the excess lining fabric twice by about 1.5cm (⅝in) over the top edge of the bag and tack in place, catching in the border lace and the handle loops. Topstitch in place. Sew the buttons to the lace on the front of the bag beneath the loops for the handles. Remove any remaining tacking stitches.

Spring is in the Air

Embroidered bag   **Size:** approximately 18 x 22cm (7 x 8¾in)   Pattern sheet A

Level of difficulty ♡ ♡

Materials

Cotton fabric, about 110cm (44in) wide:
- 10cm (4in) fabric with diagonal stripes
- 15cm (6in) colourful floral fabric
- 10cm (4in) pink spotted fabric
- 25cm (10in) blue spotted fabric
- 10cm (4in) white fabric for the embroidery

Wadding:
- 30 x 90cm (12 x 35½in) fusible wadding

Additional items:
- 55cm (21¾in) coordinating rickrack braid, 10mm (⅜in) wide
- 6-strand embroidery cotton in brown, light pink, pink, rust red, yellow and turquoise
- 4 brown buttons, 20mm (¾in) diameter
- 1 press-stud, 15mm (⅝in) diameter
- iron-on transfer pen
- tissue paper or greaseproof paper

Cutting out

The following measurements include a 0.75cm (¼in) seam allowance.

Striped fabric:
- 2 strips 5 x 21.5cm (2 x 8½in)

Floral fabric:
- 2 strips 5 x 21.5cm (2 x 8½in)
- 4 strips 5.5 x 45cm (2¼ x 17¾in) for handles

Pink spotted fabric:
- 2 strips 5 x 21.5cm (2 x 8½in)
- 1 rectangle 7.5 x 11cm (3 x 4¼in) for the tab closure

Blue spotted fabric:
- 2 strips 3.5 x 21.5cm (1¼ x 8½in)
- 2 strips 4 x 21.5cm (1½ x 8½in)
- 4 strips 4 x 22.5cm (1½ x 9in) for the sides
- 2 rectangles 21.5 x 25.5cm (8½ x 10in) for lining

White fabric:
- 2 strips 10 x 25cm (4 x 10in) for the embroidery on the bag front/back
- 1 rectangle 10 x 15cm (4 x 6in) for the embroidery on the tab

Fusible wadding:
- 2 rectangles 21 x 25cm (8¼ x 10in)
- 4 strips 4 x 43.5cm (1½ x 17in) for the handles
- 1 rectangle 6 x 9.5cm (2¼ x 3¾in) for the tab

Sewing

1 Sew two identical sets of strips with right sides facing, joining them along the 21.5cm (8½in) edges in the following order from top to bottom: blue spotted, pink spotted, floral, white, striped, blue spotted.

2 With right sides facing, pin a 22.5cm (9in) blue spotted strip along each side edge of each set of strips. Stitch in place. Iron a rectangle of wadding to the back of each set of strips. Topstitch the ric-rac braid on top, centred on the seam line between the pink fabric and the floral one. Quilt all the seams by stitching in the ditch (sewing along the seams) or as desired. Lay the two quilted pieces right sides together and sew together around the sides and lower edge. Shape the base as explained on page 11.

3 Pin the blue lining rectangles right sides together and stitch the short sides and lower edge, leaving a gap in the base seam for turning out.

4 Fuse the small wadding rectangle to the back of the embroidered tab piece. Now tack the embroidery right sides together with the small pink spotted rectangle. Trim the corners at one end to round them off. Sew together all round, leaving the short straight edge open. Turn right sides out and press.

5 Iron the wadding centrally on to the wrong side of each floral handle strip. Round off the corners on each one, using a template or tracing around a suitable round object (see the diagram and instructions on page 11). Pin the strips together in pairs with right sides facing and sew around the edge, leaving a gap in the seam along one long edge for turning out. Turn out, press and topstitch close to the edge all round. Fold the centre 17cm (6¾in) of each strip in half lengthways and sew together to shape the handle.

Assembly

1 Place the bag inside the lining with right sides facing, placing the tab in the centre of the top edge between the two layers. Sew together all round. Turn the bag out through the opening in the lining, press and topstitch close to the top edge, folding the tab out of the way of the stitching. Close up the opening in the lining with small hand stitches.

2 Attach the ends of the handles to the bag with a button, positioning them an equal distance from the sides. Attach one part of the press-stud to the underneath of the tab and the other to the corresponding area on the body of the bag to finish.

Preparation

Trace the embroidery pattern on to tissue paper or greaseproof paper using the iron-on transfer pen. The pattern is given in mirror image so that it will be the right way round when you transfer it to your fabric. Lay the pattern on to the right side of each long white fabric strip and iron to transfer the design. For the tab, just transfer half of the embroidery template on to the fabric.

Embroidery

Embroider the butterfly bodies in brown and their wings in turquoise using backstitch. Embroider the line of flight in brown using running stitch and the flowers in light pink, pink and rust red using lazy daisy stitch. Mark the centre of each flower with a single yellow French knot. When the embroidery is complete, trim the embroidered fabrics for the front/back to 7.5 x 21.5cm (3 x 8½in) and the one for the tab to 7.5 x 11cm (3 x 4¼in).

Sea Breeze

Elegant shopper   **Size:** approximately 33cm (13in) high   **Level of difficulty** ♡

Materials

Batik fabric, about 110cm (44in) wide:
- 15cm (6in) each of 7 different batik fabrics in blue/purple/green
- 55cm (21¾in) matching batik fabric for the lining
- scraps of colourful fabric for the rosettes

Wadding:
- 50 x 114cm (19¾ x 45in) sew-in wadding

Additional items:
- 1 karabiner (swivel key holder)
- 1 sew-on magnetic press-stud
- coordinating decorative buttons

Preparation

Select a strip for the handles from your main fabrics and cut two strips 12 x 50cm (4¾ x 19¾in).

Cutting out

The following measurements include a 0.75cm (¼in) seam allowance.

Assorted batik fabrics:
- strips 80cm (31½in) long in different widths
- 4 strips 6 x 10cm (2¼ x 4in) for the loops

Lining fabric:
- 50 x 80cm (19¾ x 31½in) for the bag lining
- 1 strip 4 x 25cm (1½ x 10in) for a key loop

Wadding:
- 50 x 80cm (19¾ x 31½in) rectangle
- 2 strips 4 x 50cm (1½ x 19¾in) for the handles

Joining the strips

Lay the wadding rectangle on the work surface. Lay the first strip of batik fabric right side up on top, matching one 80cm (31½in) edge. Lay the second strip of fabric on top of the first, right sides together and sew through all layers, using the width of the presser foot as a guide. Fold back the top strip of fabric and iron, so that the right side of the fabric is visible. Repeat this process until the whole of the wadding rectangle is covered with strips of fabric. To prevent the rectangle from losing its shape, alternate the sewing direction, i.e. sew from the top down then from the bottom up. Fold the completed rectangle in half, right sides together so that it is 40 x 50cm (15¾ x 19¾in) and close up the side seams.

To cut the circles for the rosettes, use a round plastic template or draw around a glass or other round object.

Sewing

1 Iron the bag, pressing the bottom fold to mark the centre of the base, or draw a line on the wadding side. Push one side seam towards the inside on to the base fold or line. This will form a triangle at the side (see page 11). Stitch across the triangle at right angles to the seam, 10cm (4in) away from the point. Trim off the excess fabric to leave a small seam allowance and zigzag the edges together. Repeat on the other side to shape the bag base.

2 Sew together the lining as for the outer bag, leaving a gap in a side seam for turning out. Shape the base as before.

3 Press 1cm (⅜in) to the wrong side along one long edge of each handle strip. Lay a strip of wadding centred on the wrong side of the strip. First fold the unfinished long edge over on to the wadding and then fold the ironed long edge over the top, so that the fabric edges overlap. Topstitch close to the folded edge through all the layers. Work a second line of topstitching an even distance away to secure the layers further and for decoration.

4 Fold the key-loop strip in half lengthways, right sides together, and sew the open long edge together. Turn the strip right sides out. Arrange the long seam so that it is in the centre and press. Fold the strip so the ends meet with the long seam in the middle. Slip the karabiner hook on to the loop.

Assembly

1 Place the lining into the bag, right sides together. Lay the key loop and the ends of the handles between the layers of fabric so that the raw edges are level and the main part of each handle is between the fabric layers. Place the key loop at the side and the ends of the handles about 12cm (4¾in) away from the side seams. Sew the top edge of the bag and then turn the bag out through the opening in the lining. Close up the opening with small hand stitches and push the lining into the bag. Topstitch the top of the bag 1cm (⅜in) from the edge.

2 For the button rosettes, cut several circles with different diameters from the remnants of fabric. Roll a small hem to the wrong side of each circle and work running stitch along the turning using a matching double thread (see page 11). Pull up the thread to gather the fabric then flatten the fabric into a circle and even out the folds. Tie off the thread ends and use them to sew the rosette, together with a decorative button, to the bag.

3 Sew the two sections of the magnetic press-stud inside the bag at the centre of the top edge to close it.

If you want to make inside pockets from the fabric remnants, they must be sewn to the right side of the lining before the lining is secured to the bag.

Materials

Cotton fabric:
- 💜 80cm (1yd) red fabric with white spots, about 110cm (44in) wide, for the bag and lining
- 💜 8.5 x 4–9cm (3¼ x 1½–3½in) strips cut from about 16 different blue-and-white fabric remnants

Wadding and interfacing:
- 💜 40 x 90cm (16 x 35½in) fusible wadding
- 💜 11 x 30cm (4¼ x 12in) firm fusible interfacing

Additional items:
- 💜 2 circular bamboo bag handles, about 15cm (6in) in diameter

Cutting out

The following measurements include a 0.75cm (¼in) seam allowance.

Spotted fabric:
- 💜 2 strips 8.5 x 45.5cm (3½ x 18in) for the upper section
- 💜 2 rectangles 19.5 x 45.5cm (7¾ x 18in) for the lower section
- 💜 2 rectangles 33.5 x 45.5cm (13¼ x 18in) for the lining

Blue-and-white fabrics:
- 💜 about 16 rectangles, each 8.5cm (3½in) wide, but in different lengths, e.g. 4–9cm (1½–3½in)
- 💜 4 handle holders from pattern sheet A

Fusible wadding:
- 💜 2 rectangles 33.5 x 45.5cm (13¼ x 18in)

Summer Spots

Bag with bamboo   Size: 25 x 42cm (10 x 16½in)   Pattern sheet A

Level of difficulty ♡

Preparation

Make a template for the handle holders using the pattern on sheet A. Add a 0.75cm (¼in) seam allowance all round.

Sewing

1 With right sides facing, sew the blue-and-white fabrics together along the 8.5cm (3½in) edges to make two strips about 50cm (19¾in) long. Sew each strip, right sides together, between one upper bag section and one lower bag section. Iron the wadding on to the wrong side of each of the new rectangles. Lay these rectangles right sides together and stitch the sides and bottom edge.

2 Lay the two lining rectangles right sides together and stitch the bottom seam. Press the seam flat. Iron the firm interfacing centred on the wrong side of the base seam of the lining. Fold the lining right sides together and close up the side seams, leaving a gap in one seam for turning out.

3 To shape the base, push one side seam of the main bag on to the bottom seam, creating a triangle at the end (see page 11). Stitch at right angles to the seam, 6cm (2½in) away from the corner point. Trim off the excess fabric to leave a small seam allowance and zigzag the raw edges together. Repeat on the other side seam and on the lining.

Assembly

1 Place the lining into the bag, right sides together, with edges and seams matching. Sew along the top edge. Turn out through the opening in the lining, push out the seams carefully and press. Close up the opening in the lining with small hand stitches.

2 Place the handle holders together in pairs with right sides facing and stitch together all round, leaving one end open for turning out. Turn the holders right sides out, turn in the open short edges by the width of the seam allowance and press. Close up the opening by hand. Centre each handle holder on the bag, about 1.5cm (⅝in) below the top edge (see the photograph). Topstitch close to the shorter curved edge. Push the bamboo handle under the holder and topstitch the longer curved edge of the holder, sewing close to the edge.

Favourite Wash Bag

Cosmetic purse   **Size:** approximately 37cm (14½in) high   Pattern sheet A

Level of difficulty ♡ ♡

Materials

Cotton fabric, 110cm (44in) wide:
- 50cm (½yd) large-pattern fabric
- 50 x 55cm (19¾ x 21¾in) green fabric for the trimming
- 20cm (8in) white fabric for the lining

Wadding:
- 25 x 90cm (10 x 35½in) fusible wadding

Additional items:
- 1 open-ended zip fastener in beige, 80cm (31½in) long
- 1 zip pull

Preparation

Make a template for the centre and sides using the patterns on sheet A. A seam allowance of 0.75cm (¼in) is included on both patterns.

Cutting out

The following measurements include a 0.75cm (¼in) seam allowance.

Large-pattern fabric:
- 1 centre panel cut on the fold
- 2 side panels cut on the fold
- 1 rectangle 17 x 19cm (6¾ x 7½in) for the inside pocket

Green fabric:
- 4 strips 4.5 x 18cm (1¾ x 7in) for trimming
- several 6.5cm (2½in) strips cut on the bias (at a 45° angle) from the remaining fabric for binding. Join the strips along the short ends to make a long strip at least 80cm (31½in) long.

White fabric:
- 1 centre panel cut on the fold
- 2 side panels cut on the fold
- 1 rectangle 5 x 7cm (2 x 2¾in) for the zip cover

Fusible wadding:
- 1 centre panel cut on the fold (or see the note on page 32)
- 2 side panels cut on the fold

Sewing

1 Fold the pocket piece lengthways, right sides together, and sew along the 19cm (7½in) edge. Turn out the pocket, arrange the seam so that it is in the centre back and press well. Topstitch close to the long edges. The short sides remain unfinished – these will later be caught in the seam between the centre and the side panels.

2 Fold the four green trimming strips in half lengthways, wrong sides together, and press neatly. Fuse wadding to the wrong side of the main pattern pieces (see note below). Now tack a folded trimming strip to the long diagonal edges of each side panel, matching the raw edges. Pin this edge to the corresponding side edge of the centre panel and stitch in place, beginning the stitching at the top edge and ending at the place marked on the pattern, 0.75cm (¼in) from the end of the seam. Finally, close up the bottom edge of the bag.

3 Pin the pocket on one side of a centre lining panel and topstitch the bottom edge in place (see the line on the pattern for placement). Join the lining pieces as for the bag but omitting the trimming strips and catching the inside pocket in the side-panel seams.

4 Press 0.75cm (¼in) to the wrong side all around the 5 x 7cm (2 x 2¾in) zip cover and sew the rectangle to the bag lining on three sides, as indicated on the pattern. The top edge remains open. The zip tab will go here later. Put the lining into the bag, wrong sides together.

5 Measure the length of the top edge of the bag and cut the 6.5cm (2½in) bias binding to the required length plus seam allowances. Sew the short ends together to make a ring and then press the binding in half, wrong sides together. Tack the top edge of the lining to the top edge of the bag, making sure that the trimming strips are pressed towards the sides. Pin and sew on the binding, aligning the raw edges with the top of the bag on the lining side. Remove all tacking stitches. Turn the bag right side out, turn the binding over to the front and pin in place, covering the previous stitching line. Do not stitch in place yet.

6 You only need half of the zip. Tack the zip fastener from the inside to the bias binding, beginning on the side where the zip cover is, leaving the zip to overlap by about 5cm (2in) at the ends. Using the zipper foot on your machine, sew the bias binding close to the edge, catching in the zip fastener at the same time. Do not stitch down the zip fastener in the area of the cover. Attach the zip pull on to the zip fastener, push the ends of the zip fastener into the cover and sew up the remaining open edge by hand.

Fuse the wadding to the back of your large-print fabric before cutting out the pattern pieces. This makes the fusing process easier and helps to avoid getting glue from the wadding on the iron or ironing board.

Red Retro

Holdall   Size: approximately 30cm (12in) high   Pattern sheet A

Level of difficulty ♡ ♡

Materials

Cotton fabric, about 280cm (110in) wide:
- 50cm (½yd) red–and-cream striped fabric
- 50cm (½yd) red-and-cream fabric with motifs, such as the toile de jouy fabric shown
- 25cm (¼yd) coordinating fabric for the bag straps and inside pocket

Wadding and interfacing:
- 130 x 90cm (51 x 35½in) fusible wadding
- 130 x 90cm (51 x 35½in) firm fusible pelmet interfacing

Additional items:
- 120cm (47in) white lace trimming, 12mm (½in) wide
- 5cm (2in) hook-and-loop tape, such as Velcro
- 4 clip-together curtain eyelets
- 1 cream open-ended zip fastener, 45cm (18in) long
- 1 zip pull

Preparation

Make a template for the top panel and round off the corners following the patterns. A seam allowance of 0.75cm (¼in) is included.

Cutting out

The following measurements include a 0.75cm (¼in) seam allowance.

Striped fabric:
- 4 top panels cut on the fold
- 1 rectangle 25 x 55cm (10 x 21¾in) for the inside pocket
- 2 strips 6 x 135cm (2⅜ x 53in) for the handles

Toile de jouy fabric:
- 4 rectangles 30 x 55cm (12 x 21¾in) for the bag and lining
- 2 strips 6 x 135cm (2⅜ x 53in) for the handles
- 2 strips 5 x 25cm (2 x 10in) for the pocket flap

Coordinating fabric:
- 2 rectangles 15 x 25cm (6 x 10in) for the inside pocket
- 4 strips 12 x 36cm (4¾ x 14in) for the zip placket
- 2 strips 6 x 135cm (2⅜ x 53in) for the handles

Fusible wadding:
- 2 strips 20 x 58cm (8 x 22¾in) for the top panel
- 2 rectangles 30 x 55cm (12 x 21¾in) for the main bag
- 2 strips 12 x 36cm (4¾ x 14in) for the zip placket

Firm iron-on pelmet interfacing:
- 2 strips 20 x 58cm (8 x 22¾in) for the top panel
- 2 rectangles 30 x 55cm (12 x 21¾in) for the main bag
- 2 strips 12 x 36cm (4¾ x 14in) for the zip placket

Sewing the top panel

1 Sew together two of the four top panels along the short sides to form a ring. Iron a 20 x 58cm (8 x 22¾in) piece of wadding and then firm interfacing to the wrong side of each of the other two top-panel pieces. Quilt the wadded pieces as desired, perhaps by quilting along the red stripes at regular intervals. Trim the wadding to the size of the fabric pieces. To prevent the layers from slipping, sew the pieces together around the edge with zigzag stitch.

2 Now sew the quilted top-panel pieces together to form a ring. Put one top-panel ring inside the other, right sides together, and carefully sew together along the curved top edge, using the width of the presser foot as a guide. Before turning out, clip the seam allowance in the curves up to the seam so the fabric will lie flat when turned out (see page 10). Turn out the top panel and topstitch close to the curved edge. Neaten the bottom, straight edges together with zigzag stitch. Insert the eyelets in the positions marked on the pattern, following the manufacturer's instructions.

Sewing

1 Iron the corresponding wadding and interfacing pieces to the wrong side of two of the four toile de jouy rectangles and quilt as desired. Put the two quilted rectangles right sides together and stitch both 30cm (12in) side seams. Turn right sides out. Arrange the top panel over the bag, right sides together, aligning the side seams and straight edges. Sew together using the width of the presser foot as a guide.

2 Take two of the four fabric strips for the zip placket and fuse a corresponding strip of wadding and interfacing to the back of each one. Place an unpadded zip placket right sides together with one padded placket strip. Lay the zip between the layers of fabric, flush with one long edge, with the teeth of the zip fastener facing the padded piece on the inside. Sew in the zip using a zipper foot. Turn the fabric right side out so the teeth of the zip fastener are visible, press and topstitch close to the edge of the zip teeth. Quilt as desired. Repeat to attach the remaining placket pieces to the other side of the zip. Put the zip pull on to the zip and round off the corners of the placket as shown on the pattern sheet. Neaten the edges together with zigzag stitch. Attach the placket to the top of the bag where it meets the top panel.

3 Turn the bag wrong side out, leaving the zip open a little way so you will be able to turn the bag right sides out after stitching. Sew together the base seam that is still open, taking a 1cm (⅜in) seam allowance.

4 To shape the base of the bag, push one side seam to the inside on to the base seam. This will form a triangle at the sides (see page 11). Stitch at right angles across the seam through all layers, 12cm (4¾in) from the point. Trim off the excess fabric to leave a small seam allowance and zigzag over the raw edges. Repeat on the other side seam. Turn the bag out, fold the fabric between the newly stitched ends and topstitch close to the fold to mark the shape the base. Make sure your fold lines are parallel.

5 Stitch a pocket-flap rectangle to each side of the striped pocket piece with right sides facing. Press the seams open. Fold the new rectangle in half with right sides together, matching the seams. The coordinating fabric will form a top flap. Stitch the open edges together all round, leaving a gap in the seam on one long side for turning out. Turn the pocket out, pushing the seams out carefully at the corners. Press the pocket and topstitch close to the edge all round, closing up the opening for turning as you do so. Press the bottom end of the pocket over to meet the flap fabric and fold the flap over the top. Press again. Sew a length of hook-and-loop tape to the inside of the flap to hold the pocket closed. Stitch the other piece to the pocket to correspond. Sew the pocket centred on the right side of one of the lining sections, stitching around the sides and lower edge of the pocket. You can also secure the top of the pocket under the flap.

6 Stitch the two remaining bag rectangles together with right sides facing along both 30cm (12in) edges and the bottom edge. Shape the corners of the base as you did for the outer bag, but do not topstitch the base afterwards. Press the seam allowance at the top edge of the lining over to the wrong side. Now place the lining into the bag with wrong sides facing and hand stitch the lining to the zip placket, enclosing the raw edges.

7 For the handles, make a plait using one strip of each of your three fabrics. Repeat with the remaining three strips then trim both plaits to the same length. Push the ends of the plaits through the eyelets and tie them firmly.

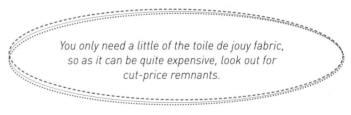

You only need a little of the toile de jouy fabric, so as it can be quite expensive, look out for cut-price remnants.

Fun and Flirty

Happy-go-lucky clutch bag   **Size:** approximately 21cm (8¼in) high   Pattern sheet A

Level of difficulty ♡

Materials

Cotton fabric, about 110cm (44in) wide:
- 45cm (½yd) light blue floral fabric
- 40cm (16in) red-and-white checked fabric

Wadding and interfacing:
- 40 x 90cm (16 x 35½in) fusible wadding
- 40 x 90cm (16 x 35½in) firm fusible pelmet interfacing

Additional item:
- circular metal clip handle

Preparation

Make a template for the bag using the pattern on sheet A. Add a 1cm (⅜in) seam allowance all round.

Cutting out

The following measurements include a 1cm (⅜in) seam allowance for the inside pocket and the channel for the handles and a 2cm (¾in) hem.

Blue floral fabric:
- 2 bag pieces cut on the fold
- 1 strip 15 x 80cm (6 x 31½in) for the base/sides
- 2 strips 8 x 32cm (3¼ x 12½in) for the handle channel

Red checked fabric:
- 2 bag pieces cut on the fold for the lining
- 1 strip 15 x 80cm (6 x 31½in) for the base/side lining
- 1 rectangle 20 x 30cm (8 x 12in) for the inside pocket

Fusible wadding:
- 2 bag pieces cut on the fold
- 1 strip 15 x 80cm (6 x 31½in) for the base/sides

Firm fusible pelmet interfacing:
- 2 bag pieces cut on the fold
- 1 strip 15 x 80cm (6 x 31½in) for the base/sides

Sewing

1 Back all the floral bag pieces, except for the strips for the handle channel, by ironing on the corresponding fusible wadding and back all the red checked pieces, except for the inside pocket, by ironing on the corresponding interfacing.

2 Fold the pocket rectangle in half widthways with right sides facing so it is 20 x 15cm (8 x 6in) and sew together the open edges, leaving a gap in the seam on one side for turning out. Trim the seam allowances at the corners (see page 11). Turn out the pocket, pushing out the corners carefully, and close up the opening with small hand stitches. Topstitch the pocket on one long edge, using the presser foot as a guide – this will be the top edge. Pin the pocket centrally to the right side of one bag lining then stitch it in place around the sides and bottom edge.

3 Now stitch the wadded base/side piece to one wadded bag piece and then to the other so it is in the middle. Stitch these seams with right sides facing and raw edges matching.

4 Assemble the lining pieces in the same way, but leave a gap in one seam for turning out. Make sure the stitches are secured on either side of the gap. Turn the lining right side out.

5 Hem each of the two short channel strips by turning the edges of the fabric to the wrong side twice by 1cm (⅜in) and sewing in place. Fold each strip in half lengthways, wrong sides together, and topstitch 2.5cm (1in) from the fold and parallel to it. With right sides facing, centre each channel on the wadded front and back pieces, flush to the top raw edge.

Assembly

Place the lining into the bag, right sides together, matching the raw edges. Sew along the top edge, catching in the channels for the handles at the same time. Turn the bag out through the opening in the lining and close up the opening with small hand stitches. Push the lining into the bag. Topstitch the edge of the bag using the width of the presser foot as a guide.

Adding the handles

Guide the long pins of the bag handles through the channels, place the screws on the ends and tighten up.

Dynamic Duo

Shoulder bag   **Size:** 17 x 15cm (6¾ x 6in)   Pattern sheet A   **Level of difficulty** ♡

Materials

Cotton fabric, about 110cm (44in) wide:
- 60cm (¾yd) white fabric with a cherry design

Wadding and interfacing:
- 25cm (10in) lightweight fusible wadding
- 20 x 90cm (8 x 35½in) fusible interfacing

Additional items:
- 2 karabiner hooks (swivel key holders), 4cm (1½in) long
- 1 white zip fastener, 25cm (10in) long
- matching or coordinating bias binding about 1.5m (1½yd) long (optional)
- tailor's chalk or an erasable fabric marker pen

Cutting out

The following measurements include a 0.75cm (¼in) seam allowance.

Cherry fabric:
- 4 bag pieces for the bag and lining
- 1 strip 4.5 x 66.5cm (1¾ x 26¼in) for the handles
- 1 strip 5.5 x 16.5cm (2¼ x 6½in) for the karabiner loops

Lightweight fusible wadding:
- 2 bag pieces

Fusible interfacing:
- 1 strip 4.5 x 66.5cm (1¾ x 26¼in) for the handles

Preparation

Make a template for the bag using the pattern on sheet A. Add a seam allowance of 0.75cm (¼in) all round.

Sewing

1 Fuse wadding to the wrong side of two bag pieces. Draw on a grid of diagonal lines at 2.5cm (1in) intervals and hand quilt along the lines using running stitch.

2 Place the zip right sides together with the top edge of one quilted bag piece. Place an unquilted (lining) piece on top, right side down, and sew together close to the zip teeth. Open out so the lining and quilted piece are wrong sides together. Press and then topstitch along the zip on the right side, close to the teeth. Repeat for the other side of the zip. Machine zigzag around the edges of the layers to hold them in place. They will be now be used as one piece.

3 Fold and stitch the strip for the karabiner loops as described for a strap on page 11. Topstitch the long sides close to the edge. Cut the strip into two equal pieces and then fold each one in half so the ends meet to make a loop. Sew one loop to each end of the zip.

4 Stitch the base of the bag together with right sides facing. Enclose the raw edges of the stitched seam on the inside with bias binding, if using. Join the seams A1 to A2 on each side and again enclose the seam allowances with bias binding. Next join B1 to B2 on each side and enclose the raw edges with bias binding, if using.

Making the strap

1 Iron interfacing to the wrong side of the strap fabric. Fold under a seam allowance all round and press. Fold the strap in half lengthways with wrong sides facing, matching the folded edges, and topstitch around the edge.

2 Thread each end of the strap through a karabiner ring, fold the end over on itself and sew down. Use the karabiner hooks to attach the strap to the loops on the sides of the bag.

Mobile-phone case

Size: 6.5 x 11cm (2½ x 4¼in)   **Level of difficulty** ♡

Materials

Cotton fabric, about 110cm (44in) wide:
- ♥ 40 x 50cm (16 x 19¾in) white fabric with a cherry design

Wadding:
- ♥ 8.5 x 21.5cm (3¼ x 8½in)

Additional items:
- ♥ press-stud fastening
- ♥ tailor's chalk or an erasable fabric marker pen

Cutting out

The following measurements include a 0.75cm (¼in) seam allowance.

Cherry fabric:
- ♥ 2 strips 8.5 x 21.5cm (3¼ x 8½in) for the case and lining
- ♥ 1 strip 4 x 13.5cm (1½ x 5¼in) for the tab

Sewing

1 Fuse the wadding to the back of one fabric strip and draw on a grid of diagonal lines at 2.5cm (1in) intervals using tailor's chalk or an erasable marker pen. Hand quilt along the lines using running stitch.

2 Fold the tab strip in half widthways, right sides facing and sew the side seams together; turn out. Place the tab on the quilted case rectangle so that the open end is centred on one short edge of the case with raw edges matching. Tack the tab in place.

3 Fold the quilted case rectangle in half widthways, right sides together and close the side seams. Repeat with the unquilted case piece (lining), leaving a gap of about 5cm (2in) in one seam for turning out. Put the case inside the lining, right sides together, so that the top (open) edges match, and sew around the top edge. Turn out through the opening in the lining and sew up the opening with small hand stitches. Press the case carefully.

Finishing off

Attach the top of the press-stud to the tab and determine the position of the other piece of the press-stud on the outer case, placing your phone in the case to check the fit first. Attach the other piece of the press-stud to the outer case.

On Your Travels

Laptop bag Size: approximately 35cm (13¾in) high **Level of difficulty** ♡ ♡

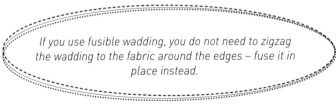

Materials

Cotton fabric, about 140cm (55in) wide:
- ♥ 35cm (½yd) brown/grey fabric in a large check
- ♥ 35 x 40cm (13¾ x 16in) brown/grey patterned fabric
- ♥ 15cm (6in) plain light brown/grey fabric for the strap backing
- ♥ 60cm (¾yd) brown/grey fabric for the lining

Wadding:
- ♥ 45 x 150cm (17¾ x 59in) wadding

Additional item:
- ♥ 34cm (13½in) hook-and-loop tape, such as Velcro

Cutting out

The following measurements include a 0.75cm (¼in) seam allowance.

Checked fabric:
- ♥ 2 rectangles 32.5 x 37.5cm (12¾ x 14¾in) for the front and back
- ♥ 2 strips 7.5 x 32.5cm (3 x 12¾in) for the sides
- ♥ 1 strip 7.5 x 37.5cm (3 x 14¾in) for the base
- ♥ 1 strip 5 x 37.5cm (2 x 14¾in) for the pocket edging

Patterned fabric:
- ♥ 1 rectangle 30 x 37.5cm (12 x 14¾in) for the bag flap

Strap backing fabric:
- ♥ 1 strip 8 x 130cm (3¼ x 51in)

Lining fabric:
- ♥ 1 strip 8 x 130cm (3¼ x 51in) for the strap
- ♥ 2 rectangles 32.5 x 37.5cm (12¾ x 14¾in) for the front/back lining
- ♥ 2 strips 7.5 x 32.5cm (3 x 12¾in) for the side linings
- ♥ 1 strip 7.5 x 37.5cm (3 x 14¾in) for the base lining
- ♥ 1 rectangle 23 x 37.5cm (9 x 14¾in) for the inside pocket
- ♥ 2 strips 10.5 x 36cm (4¼ x 14in) for fastening strips
- ♥ 1 rectangle 35 x 37.5cm (13¾ x 14¾in) for the flap facing

Wadding:
- ♥ 2 rectangles 32.5 x 37.5cm (12¾ x 14¾in) for the front/back
- ♥ 1 rectangle 34 x 37.5cm (13¾ x 14¾in) for the flap
- ♥ 2 strips 7.5 x 32.5cm (3 x 12¾in) for the sides
- ♥ 1 strip 7.5 x 37.5cm (3 x 14¾in) for the base
- ♥ 1 strip 8 x 130cm (3¼ x 51in) for the strap

If you use fusible wadding, you do not need to zigzag the wadding to the fabric around the edges – fuse it in place instead.

LE FIGA
premier quotidien nation:

NUMÉRO QUALI

Sewing

1 Lay the front, back, side and base pieces wrong side down on a corresponding piece of wadding and stitch round each one with zigzag stitch. Now stitch a side piece to each of the short edges of the base piece, beginning and ending the seams 0.75cm (¼in) away from the edges of the fabric and working with right sides facing. Sew the joined piece between the front and back pieces, again with right sides facing.

2 Pin the checked pocket edging to the pocket rectangle, matching one long edge and with the right side of the strip against the wrong side of the pocket rectangle. Stitch in place. Turn the strip over to the right side of the pocket rectangle, tuck under the seam allowance along the long edge and slipstitch it in place as if attaching binding.

3 With the edging at the top, pin the pocket to the right side of the back lining rectangle, matching the sides and bottom edges. Join the lining pieces as for the outer bag but without the wadding and quilting.

4 Pin the flap to the flap facing, with right sides facing and raw edges matching, and stitch the bottom long edge; unfold. Press the seam allowance towards the main fabric and topstitch the edge, the width of the presser foot from the seam. Fold the flap right sides together and back with a corresponding piece of wadding. Close up the flap's side seams, turn out the flap and quilt as appropriate to the design.

5 Fold each fastening strip right sides together lengthways and close up the short end seams. Turn the strips right side out and neaten the raw edges with a narrow zigzag stitch. Sew on a piece of hook and loop tape along the long folded edge.

6 Lay the strap fabric and its backing right sides together and pin these on to the corresponding piece of wadding. Sew the strap together all around, leaving a gap in one short end for turning out. Trim the seam allowance (see page 11) and trim the wadding so that it is flat. Turn out the strap, push the seam allowance inside at the opening and topstitch the strap along both long edges, following the width of the presser foot.

Assembly

Tack the flap to the back of the bag with right sides facing and pin one of the fastening strips over the top, right sides together and raw edges matching. Pin or tack the other fastening strip to the front of the bag, right sides together. Put the bag inside the lining, right sides facing and raw edges matching, and sew all around the top edge, leaving a gap in the seam in the centre front for turning out. Turn the bag out through the opening, tuck in the seam allowance at the opening and machine a narrow topstitch around the edge of the bag, closing up the opening for turning at the same time. Pin the ends of the strap to the right and left side pieces so that the strap overlaps the side by about 5cm (2in). Stitch firmly in place in a rectangle where the layers overlap and then in a cross.

Heavenly Hexagons

Patchwork bag   **Size:** 33 x 31.5cm (13 x 12½in)   Patterns sheet B

Level of difficulty ♡ ♡

Materials

Fabric:
- 40 x 90cm (16 x 35½in) natural-coloured linen
- 30 colourful remnants at least 7 x 8cm 2¾ x 3¼in)

Wadding and webbing:
- 40 x 90cm (16 x 35½in) fusible wadding
- 12 x 90cm (4¾ x 35½in) fusible webbing, such as Bondaweb

Additional items:
- 2.5m (2¾yd) pink cotton twill tape, 2cm (¾in) wide
- 2 sheets of freezer paper or firm A4 paper

Preparation

Cut out 30 hexagons from paper without adding a seam allowance, using the pattern on sheet B. If using freezer paper, iron each one on to the wrong side of a fabric remnant and cut out the fabric, adding about 0.75cm (¼in) all round for seam allowances. The seam allowances can be approximate because the paper will provide your stitching guide. If using A4 paper, pin or tack the paper in place. Make a template for the bag pattern on sheet B, adding a 0.75cm (¼in) seam allowance all round.

Cutting out

The following measurements include a 0.75cm (¼in) seam allowance.

Linen fabric:
- 4 bags cut on the fold, using the pattern on sheet B

Fusible wadding:
- 2 bags cut on the fold, using the pattern on sheet B

Pink twill tape:
- 2 pieces 15cm (6in) long
- 1 piece 170cm (67in) long

English patchwork

1 Working one edge at a time, fold the excess fabric to the back around each of the paper hexagons. Do this as neatly as possible, using the paper edges as your guide. Tack the fabric in place and press. Place the completed hexagons together in two rows of eight and two rows of seven hexagons and sew together following these steps: place two hexagons directly on top of one another, right sides together, and oversew one matching edge together, being careful not to stitch through the paper. Open out the hexagons and lay on the next hexagon. Continue like this until all the hexagons are joined together in a row.

2 Now sew one row of seven hexagons, centred, to one row of eight hexagons using the same method. Do not worry about pulling the templates a bit when doing this, as long as the edges are lying exactly on top of one another (e.g. for Y-seams). Carefully remove the tacking thread and the paper. Open out the seam allowances at the end of the last hexagons in each of the seven-hexagon rows, as indicated on the bag pattern. Trace around your strips of hexagons on the fusible webbing and cut the webbing to match. Remove the backing from the fusible webbing and iron it on to the back of each strip of hexagons.

Sewing

1 Fuse the corresponding wadding to the back of two of the linen bag pieces. These will be the front and back. Position a patchwork strip on top of each one, using the pattern as your guide, and iron in place. Topstitch each hexagon close to the edge. Pin the bag pieces together with right sides facing and sew the base and side seams. Trim any excess fabric as far as the width of the seam allowance and trim the seam allowances at an angle at the corners. Turn the bag out.

2 Sew the remaining two bag pieces together as for the outer bag, but do not turn out. This will be the lining. Push the lining into the outer bag, wrong sides together, with the top edges and side seams matching. Stitch together along the top edge, close to the edge.

Finishing off

1 Work running stitch along both straight edges at the top of the bag and pull up the thread to gather it in to 15cm (6in). Fold the three pieces of twill tape in half lengthways and firmly iron the fold line. Fold a 15cm (6in) length of tape over each of the gathered edges at the top of the bag and sew down close to the edge.

2 Starting at a side seam, use the remaining cotton twill tape to enclose one curved side edge as you did for the gathered edge. At the end, sew the long edge of the tape together for 57cm (22½in) to form a handle and then attach the tape around the other curved edge. Trim off the end of the tape, overlapping the tape that has already been sewn on and leaving about 1cm (⅜in) to tuck under as a seam allowance. Fold in the seam allowance and stitch down. Repeat on the other side of the bag.

Uniquely You

Shoulder bag   **Size:** approximately 25 x 29cm (10 x 11½in) plus the strap

Diagram on Pattern sheet B   **Level of difficulty** ♡ ♡

Materials

Cotton fabric, about 110cm (44in) wide:
- 40cm (16in) large-print fabric
- 35cm (13¾in) blue fabric with white spots
- 50cm (19¾in) pink striped fabric

Wadding:
- 40 x 114cm (16 x 45in) firm fusible wadding

Additional items:
- brown leather strap
- brown leather fastening tab

Cutting out

The following measurements include a 0.75cm (¼in) seam allowance.

Large-print fabric:
- 1 rectangle 34.5 x 79cm (13¾ x 31in) for the bag
- 1 rectangle 15 x 34cm (6 x 13½in) for the inner pocket

Spotted fabric:
- 4 rectangles 15.5 x 34.5cm (6¼ x 13¾in) for the flap, tapered to produce two mirrored pairs following the diagrams on sheet B

Striped fabric:
- 1 strip 6.5 x 67.5cm (2½ x 26½in) for the binding
- 2 rectangles 34.5 x 39.5cm (13¾ x 15½in) for the lining

Sewing

1 Fold the pocket rectangle in half, with right sides facing, to form a 15 x 17cm (6 x 6¾in) piece and then sew up the three open sides, leaving an opening for turning. Turn the pocket out, close up the opening by hand and pin it centrally on to one of the two striped rectangles, so it is 8cm (3¼in) above the bottom edge. Sew around the pocket, leaving the top edge open.

2 Sew a tapered spotted bag piece to each short edge of the large-print bag rectangle, with right sides facing and with the longer side edge of the spotted fabric facing to the same side at each end. Fuse the wadding to the back and trim to match. Fold the fabric in half, right sides together, so that the spotted end pieces match. Sew the seams on both sides, including on the spotted fabric.

3 Mark the centre of the bag base by pressing a fold. Push one side seam over the fold at the base of the bag so that a triangle is formed at the side (see page 11). Stitch across the triangle at right angles to the seam, 8cm (3¼in) away from the point. Repeat on the opposite side. Fold each of the triangles down on to the base, holding in place with a stitch, if necessary.

4 Stitch the two striped rectangles together along one short edge with right sides facing. Unfold and attach a tapered spotted piece to each end as you did for the bag. Refold and stitch the side seams. Shape the corners of the base as you did for the bag.

Binding and finishing

1 Press the binding strips as described for a strap on page 11.

2 Put the lining inside the bag, wrong sides together, with seams and edges matching. Check the fit of the binding strip around the top of the bag and then unfold and stitch the ends together with right sides facing to form a ring. With the binding unfolded, pin one long edge to the open edge of the bag with right sides facing. Stitch in place, along the first fold. Fold the binding over to the lining side, tuck in the long edge and sew it in place by hand.

3 Sew on the leather strap and fastening, using the photograph as a guide for positioning the fastening.

Just for Fun

Casual bag   Size: approximately 43 x 34cm (17 x 13½in)   Pattern sheet B

Level of difficulty ♡ ♡

Materials

Cotton fabric, about 140cm (55in) wide:
- 50cm (½yd) bold-print fabric
- 50cm (½yd) contrasting spotted fabric for the lining

Wadding:
- 60 x 114cm (23½ x 45in) firm sew-in wadding

Additional item:
- circle template, 12.5cm (5in) diameter

Cutting out

The following measurements include a 0.75cm (¼in) seam allowance. When cutting out the pieces, ensure that large motifs are centred on the front and back of the bag as far as possible.

Bold-print fabric:
- 2 bags cut on the fold
- 1 bag base cut on the fold
- 4 strips 5.5 x 60cm (2¼ x 23½in) for handles

Spotted fabric:
- 2 bags cut on the fold
- 1 bag base cut on the fold

Firm wadding:
- 2 bags cut on the fold
- 1 bag base cut on the fold
- 2 strips 4 x 60cm (1½ x 23½in) for the handles

Preparation

Make a template for the bag and the base using the patterns on sheet B. Add a 0.75cm (¼in) seam allowances all round.

Sewing

1 Tack the corresponding wadding to the wrong side of the three bold-print bag pieces and quilt as desired. In the example shown in the photograph, the pieces were quilted around the large motifs and where the colour blocks change. If you cannot find a fabric like the one shown, you can always appliqué your own motifs on the bag pieces before quilting (see page 12).

2 Lay the two quilted bag shapes right sides together and stitch the side seams with right sides facing. Attach the quilted base, matching the marks at the ends on the pattern with the side seams. Repeat to join the spotted lining pieces to each other but leave a gap in one side seam for turning out.

3 Fold the seam allowances on the four bold-print handle strips to the wrong side and press well. Lay out two of the strips, wrong side up, and place a wadding strip on top of each one, tucking it under the pressed seam allowances. Pin a second strip wrong side down on top and topstitch the handles along the long edges, close to the edge. Topstitch the handles three or four more times at equal intervals along the length.

Assembly

Place the bag in the lining with right sides facing, matching seams and the top edge. Place the handles between the layers of fabric so the ends match the raw edges of the bag and lining 8cm (3¼in) away from the side seams. Sew the bag together along the top edge, catching in the handles at the same time. Turn the bag out through the opening in the lining and close up the opening with small hand stitches. Arrange the lining inside the bag and topstitch the top edge following the width of the presser foot.

Rosettes

Make rosettes from the remnants of fabric following the instructions on page 11 and attach these to the bag where they suit the pattern of the fabric.

Rose Windows

Large holdall   **Size:** approximately 45 x 46cm (17¾ x 18in)   **Level of difficulty** ♡ ♡

Materials

Cotton fabric, about 110cm (44in) wide:
- A: 10cm (4in) rose fabric with blue background
- B: 10cm (4in) rose fabric with red background
- C: 10 x 55cm (4 x 21½in) fabric with small roses
- D: 10 x 55cm (4 x 21½in) fabric with large roses
- E: 50cm (20in) blue fabric for the sides and borders
- F: 40cm (16in) red fabric for borders and binding
- G: 70cm (27½in) coordinating fabric for lining

Wadding and interfacing:
- 35 x 90cm (13¾ x 35½in) lightweight fusible wadding
- 100 x 90cm (39½ x 35½in) heavyweight fusible wadding
- 10 x 48cm (4 x 19in) lightweight fusible pelmet interfacing

Additional items:
- pair of blue leather bag handles 70cm (27½in) long
- straight patchwork ruler, rotary cutter and self-healing cutting mat

Fabrics A–D are cut into 9cm (3½in) squares. You need 24 squares in all so you could use a charm pack of coordinated fabrics for these, cutting the 12.5cm (5in) squares down to size.

Cutting out

The following measurements include a 0.75cm (¼in) seam allowance.

Fabric A:
- 10 squares 9 x 9cm (3½ x 3½in)

Fabric B:
- 6 squares 9 x 9cm (3½ x 3½in)

Fabric C:
- 4 squares 9 x 9cm (3½ x 3½in)

Fabric D:
- 4 squares 9 x 9cm (3½ x 3½in)

Fabric E:
- 10 strips 3.5 x 110cm (1⅜ x 43½in) for borders
- 2 strips 12 x 42cm (4¾ x 16½in) for the bag sides

Fabric F:
- 4 strips 4.5 x 50cm (1¾ x 19¾in)
- 4 strips 4.5 x 42cm (1¾ x 16½in)
- 18 strips 4.5 x 15cm (1¾ x 6in)
- 1 strip 4 x 135cm (1½ x 53in), joining pieces as necessary to make up the length
- 4 strips 3.5 x 25cm (1⅜ x 10in) for the ties

Fabric G:
- 2 rectangles 42 x 48cm (16½ x 19in) for the front/back lining
- 2 strips 12 x 42cm (4¾ x 16½in) for the side lining
- 2 strips 12 x 48cm (4¾ x 19in) for the base and base lining

Lightweight fusible wadding:
- 18 strips 4.5 x 15cm (1¾ x 6in)
- 4 strips 4.5 x 42cm (1¾ x 16½in)
- 1 strip 4 x 90cm (1½ x 35½in)
- 1 strip 4 x 45cm (1½ x 17¾in)

Sewing

1 Fold each of the four tie strips (fabric F) lengthways, right sides together, and sew together along the long open edge. Turn the strips out, tuck in the seam allowance at one end and sew up the opening by hand.

2 Fuse a corresponding strip of wadding to the wrong side of each of the 4.5 x 42cm (1¾ x 16½in) and 4.5 x 15cm (1¾ x 6in) strips of fabric F. Fold the strips lengthways, wrong sides together, but do not iron. Place the patchwork ruler on top of each strip so that the 1.5cm (⅝in) mark is lying on the fold. Trim the folded strips to 1.5cm (⅝in) wide using the rotary cutter and cutting mat.

3 Sew a 3.5cm (1⅜in) strip from fabric E to the top and bottom and then to the left and right of each floral square, trimming the strip to length after attaching it to each side.

4 Lay out the 24 squares to make two blocks of 3 x 4 squares. Sew the squares together in rows, placing a short folded F strip between each pair so it is caught in the seam. Now join the rows with a 4.5 x 50cm (1¾ x 19¾in) strip of fabric F between the rows (see the photograph). Trim the long strips to fit as necessary then fuse heavyweight wadding to the back of each patchwork panel and trim to fit. Quilt both panels by stitching in the ditch (sewing along the seam lines).

5 Cut and fuse heavyweight wadding to the 12 x 42cm (4¾ x 16½in) bag sides (fabric E). Back one 12 x 48cm (4¾ x 19in) rectangle of fabric G first with the pelmet interfacing and then with heavyweight fusible wadding. This will be the base.

6 Lay out each patchwork panel, right side up. Pin a long folded F strip to each side edge, matching the raw edges. Pin a tie 7cm (2¾in) from the top of each side edge, matching the unfinished end to the edge of the patchwork. Tack the layers. Now stitch the patchwork panels to the sides and base, beginning and ending the stitching 0.75cm (¼in) away from the edges (Y-seams).

7 Stitch the front, back, sides and base together for the lining, leaving a gap in one of the base seams for turning out.

8 Fuse the 4cm (1½) lightweight wadding strips to the wrong side of long F strip, but leaving 1cm (⅜in) of fabric extending beyond the wadding at one end. Fold the extending fabric over the wadding and press to neaten the end. Fold the strip lengthways, wrong sides together, and pin to the top edge of the bag, matching the raw edges. Trim the strip so that the unfinished end of the strip extends 2–3cm (¾–1¼in) over the neatened end then tuck it into the neatened end of the strip. Tack the strip in place.

Assembly

Place the bag inside the lining, right sides together, with raw edges and seams matching, and sew around the top edge (where the strip is tacked in place). Turn the bag out through the opening in the lining and close up the opening with small hand stitches. Arrange the lining in the bag, so that the red F strip is even around the top. To prevent the lining from slipping, topstitch the edge of the bag around the F strip, sewing through all layers. Sew on the bag handles by hand.

Traveller's Friend

Travel holdall   **Size:** approximately 68 x 34 x 30cm (26¾ x 13½ x 12in)

Diagram on Pattern sheet A   **Level of difficulty** ♡ ♡ ♡

Materials

Cotton fabric, about 110cm (44in) wide:
- 75cm (¾yd) large-pattern floral fabric
- 50cm (½yd) petrol-blue fabric
- 50cm (½yd) brown patterned fabric
- 130cm (1½yd) brown fabric with small floral design
- 20cm (¼yd) coordinating striped fabric for handles

Wadding and interfacing:
- 140 x 90cm (55 x 35½in) patchwork interfacing with printed 60° grid (triangle)
- 140 x 90cm (55 x 35½in) patchwork interfacing with printed 90° grid (square)
- 200 x 150cm (79 x 59in) double-sided fusible wadding
- 120 x 90cm (47 x 35½in) lightweight fusible pelmet interfacing
- 110 x 30cm (43 x 12in) firm fusible pelmet interfacing
- 35 x 90cm (13¾ x 35½in) double-sided fusible webbing such as Bondaweb

Additional items:
- plate or round card template, about 12cm (4¾in) diameter
- matching, double-ended zip, 1m (39in) long
- 4 D-rings, 4cm (1½in) wide
- 4 silver foot studs
- 4 silver buttons, about 2.5cm (1in) diameter
- piping cord 4.4m (5yd) long in any colour

Cutting out

The following measurements include a 0.75cm (¼in) seam allowance.

Large-pattern fabric:
- 2 rectangles 36 x 70cm (14 x 27½in) for the front and back

Blue fabric:
- 1 rectangle 30 x 48cm (12 x 19in) for the base
- 2 rectangles 30 x 28cm (12 x 11in) for the side base
- 2 strips 8 x 110cm (3¼ x 43in) for handles and loops

Brown fabric:
- 1 rectangle 30 x 103.5cm (12 x 40¾in) for the base lining
- 4 strips 3 x 110cm (1¼ x 43in) for piping
- 2 strips 3.5 x 30cm (1½ x 12in) for the base trim

Brown floral fabric:
- 2 rectangles 36 x 70cm (14¼ x 27½in) for front and back lining
- 4 strips 14 x 100cm (5½ x 39½in) for zip placket

Striped fabric:
- 2 strips 4 x 110cm (1½ x 43in) for the handles
- 4 strips 5 x 10cm (2 x 4in) for the zip tabs

Fusible webbing:
- 5 strips 3 x 90cm (1¼ x 35½in) for the piping
- 5 strips 4 x 90cm (1½ x 35½in) for the handles

Sewing

1 Cut fusible pelmet interfacing, double-sided fusible wadding and the patchwork interfacing with 60° grid to fit the two large-pattern rectangles and fuse them to the wrong side of each fabric rectangle in that order. Quilt the four layers together, using the lines on the interfacing as a guide as follows: stitch two lines next to each other, skip one line, stitch two lines, skip one, and so on. Round off the two top corners of both pieces, using a plate or a round card template with a diameter of about 12cm (4¾in).

2 Stitch a short blue rectangle to each end of the large blue rectangle with a 3.5 x 30cm (1½ x 12in) brown strip in between. Iron the joined strip to firm pelmet interfacing, cut to fit, then lay on the double-sided fusible wadding and the patchwork interfacing with 90° grid on top, also cut to fit. Iron to fuse the layers. Quilt the fabric parallel to the long edges at 3cm (1¼in) intervals. Trim the quilted base piece at all four corners, following the diagram on sheet A (grey areas are cut off). Insert the base studs into the base of the bag on the brown strips, spaced about 8cm (3¼in) from the edges.

3 Sew a brown floral zip placket on to each long edge of the zip, using the width of the zip foot as a guide. Cut double-sided fusible wadding and lightweight pelmet interfacing to the size of the brown fabric strips and fuse to the back. Topstitch close to the zip teeth and another three times at 3cm (1¼in) intervals along the length. For the tabs that will later be attached to the ends of the zip, pin the 5 x 10cm (2 x 4in) striped rectangles together in pairs with right sides facing and sew the long edges, using the presser foot as a guide. Turn the pieces out and topstitch close to the edges. Fold the tabs in half so that the short ends match and tack one to each end of the zip.

4 Join the brown piping strips to form one long length. Iron the five 3cm (1¼in) strips from fusible webbing to the wrong side of the strip, butting the ends of the webbing together, and remove the backing paper. Fold the strips in half lengthways, place the cord in between, in the fold, and iron together. Stitch the covered cord to the front and back bag pieces, matching the raw edges, applying it up one side, along the top and down the other side. Trim the piping to length after it has been attached. Attach piping to each short end of the blue base piece.

5 On the wrong side of each long edge of the two blue handle strips, mark a 2cm (¾in) seam allowance. Iron the 4cm (1½in) strips of fusible webbing to the wrong side of the 4 x 110cm (1½ x 43in) striped strips and then fuse these on to the blue strips so that the marked seam allowance extends on each side. Turn over the side edges towards the centre on the striped side twice by 1cm (⅜in), iron and topstitch close to the edge. Trim the strips to 65cm (25½in) – the trimmings will be used to make the handle loops later. Shape the ends of each strip to a point as follows. First fold each handle in half lengthways, blue sides together, then stitch across each end, tapering to a point at the fold. Press the seam allowances flat to form a neat point. Turn the ends of the strips out.

6 For the handle loops, cut four 8cm (3¼in) pieces from the trimmings cut from the handle strips. Fold the pieces in half, matching the raw edges and with the blue fabric on the outside. Insert a D-ring into each loop. Sew these loops on to the top edge of the bag, with each loop placed 10cm (4in) from the middle.

7 Cut and fuse double-sided fusible wadding and the patchwork interfacing with the 60° grid on to the wrong side of each 36 x 70cm (14¼ x 27½in) brown floral rectangle and quilt as you did for the large floral rectangles. Round off the top corners. Prepare the two remaining zip-placket pieces and the brown strip for the base lining in the same way, but using the patchwork interfacing with 90° grid for the latter. Quilt as before. These pieces make up the lining.

Assembly

Pin the blue bag base and the zip placket, right sides together, matching the short ends, and stitch the ends to create a ring, catching in the zip tabs. Pin this to the front and back bag pieces then stitch in place. Assemble the lining pieces in the same order. Put the outer bag in the lining with right sides facing and sew together along the top edge, leaving an opening for turning. Turn the bag out, close up the opening for turning by hand and position the lining. Topstitch through all layers around the piping on the zip placket to hold the lining in place. Pass the ends of the handles through the D-rings (the two-coloured sides facing outwards), fold the points over towards the front and sew each one down with a button.

Materials

Fabrics:
- 80cm (1yd) fine linen-mix fabric with a colourful pattern
- 70cm (¾yd) red cotton fabric for lining

Wadding and interfacing:
- 55 x 90cm (21½ x 35½in) thin fusible wadding
- 20 x 90cm (8 x 35½in) soft fusible interfacing
- 20 x 30cm (8 x 12in) sturdy fusible interfacing

Additional items:
- 4 metal eyelets, 14mm (½in) diameter

Cutting out

The following measurements include a 0.75cm (¼in) seam allowance.

Linen-mix fabric:
- 2 bags
- 1 bag base
- 2 strips 7.5 x 81.5cm (3 x 32in) for the handles

Red cotton lining:
- 2 bags
- 1 bag base

Thin fusible wadding:
- 2 bags
- 1 bag base

Soft fusible interfacing:
- 2 strips, 7.5 x 81.5cm (3 x 32in) for the handles

Sturdy fusible interfacing:
- 1 bag base

Summer Bag

Summer bag   **Size:** 29 x 36cm (11½ x 14¼in) plus handles   Pattern sheet B

Level of difficulty ♡

Preparation

Make a template for the bag and base using the patterns on sheet B. Add a 0.75cm (¼in) seam allowance all round.

Sewing

1 Back the three linen bag pieces with the corresponding wadding. Make pleats in the pieces as shown on the pattern (see arrows) and tack in place. Place the two bag pieces together with right sides facing and sew the side seams. Sew in the base.

2 Make the lining in the same way, using the red bag pieces, but without the wadding. Instead, back the base lining using the sturdy fusible interfacing. When sewing the side seams together, leave a gap in one seam of about 15cm (6in) for turning out. Turn the lining to the right side.

3 Iron a soft fusible interfacing strip to the wrong side each handle strip. Iron the seam allowances at the ends of the handles to the wrong side. Fold the handles lengthways, right sides together and sew the long sides together. Turn out and iron. Topstitch the edges if desired.

Assembly

Put the outer bag in the lining with right sides facing and seams and edges matching. Stitch around the top edge and trim the seam allowance short. Turn out the bag through the opening in the lining and carefully push out the top edge. Press and then topstitch all around, close to the edge. Sew up the opening for turning in the lining with small hand stitches.

Finishing off

Attach the metal eyelets to bag at the positions marked on the pattern, following the manufacturer's instructions. Thread the handles through the eyelets and tie a knot to secure each end.

Summer Purse

Size: 10 x 15cm (4 x 6in)   Pattern sheet B   **Level of difficulty** ♡

Materials

Fabrics:
- 15cm (6in) fine linen-mix fabric with a colourful pattern
- 15cm (6in) red cotton fabric for lining

Wadding:
- 10 x 20cm (4 x 8in) lightweight fusible wadding

Additional item:
- 1 lilac zip fastener, 10cm (4in) long

Preparation

Make a template for the purse using the pattern on sheet B. Add a 0.75cm (¼in) seam allowance all round.

Cutting out

The following measurements include a 0.75cm (¼in) seam allowance.

Linen-mix fabric:
- 2 purse pieces using the pattern on sheet B

Red cotton lining:
- 2 purse pieces for the lining
- 4 strips, 3.5 x 11.5cm (1½ x 4½in) for the top band and its facing

Lightweight fusible wadding:
- 2 purse pieces
- 2 strips, 3.5 x 11.5cm (1½ x 4½in)

Sewing

1 Fuse the corresponding wadding to the wrong side of each linen-mix purse piece and two of the red strips. Work running stitch along the top edge of each linen-mix bag piece and pull up to gather the edge to 11.5cm (4½in). Secure the thread and then sew the gathered edge to a wadded red strip with right sides facing. Iron the seams towards the red band and topstitch in place along the band. Stitch the red lining the same way, but without the wadding.

2 Place the zip right sides together with the top edge of one wadded purse, place a lining piece right side down on top and tack the layers. Sew the seam. Fold the layers over, wrong sides together, press and topstitch beside the zip teeth, using the edge of the presser foot as your guide. Repeat to attach the other side of the zip fastener to the other wadded purse and lining. Open the zip fastener two thirds.

3 Arrange the purse with edges matching so that the wadded pieces are right sides together and the lining pieces are right sides together. Sew all round the edge, using the zipper foot as a guide and leaving a gap about 8cm (3in) long in the lining for turning out. Turn the bag right sides out and sew up the opening for turning by hand. Arrange the lining in the purse.

Manufacturers

The following manufacturers kindly supplied the materials and equipment used by the author. Many of these organisations provide on-line ordering facilities and distribute worldwide. However, all of the materials and equipment used in this book can be readily obtained from alternative sources, including specialist stores, on-line suppliers and mail-order companies.

Fabric

Westfalenstoffe AG, Münster, Germany
www.westfalenstoffe.de

Kurt Frowein GmbH & Co. KG, Wuppertal, Germany
www.kurt-frowein.de

Freudenberg Vliesstoffe KG, Weinheim, Germany
www.vlieseline.de

STOF A/S, Herning, Denmark
www.stof.dk

Accessories

Gütermann GmbH, Gutach-Breisgau, Germany
www.guetermann.com

Prym Consumer GmbH, Stolberg, Germany
www.prym-consumer.de

Union Knopf GmbH, Bielefeld, Germany
www.unionknopf.com